Martin Luther King Jr. Memorial

Julie Murray

Abdo
US LANDMARKS
Kids

abdopublishing.com

Published by Abdo Kids, a division of ABDO, PO Box 398166, Minneapolis, Minnesota 55439.
Copyright © 2017 by Abdo Consulting Group, Inc. International copyrights reserved in all countries.
No part of this book may be reproduced in any form without written permission from the publisher.

Printed in the United States of America, North Mankato, Minnesota.

102016

012017

 THIS BOOK CONTAINS
RECYCLED MATERIALS

Photo Credits: Getty Images, Granger Collection, iStock, ©Julie Clopper p.cover, ©Guillermo Olaizola p.17,
©Dorti p.21, ©Lissandra Melo p.22, ©kropic1 p.22, ©Steve Heap p.23 / Shutterstock.com

Production Contributors: Teddy Borth, Jennie Forsberg, Grace Hansen

Design Contributors: Christina Doffing, Candice Keimig, Dorothy Toth

Publisher's Cataloging in Publication Data

Names: Murray, Julie, author.

Title: Martin Luther King Jr. Memorial / by Julie Murray.

Description: Minneapolis, Minnesota : Abdo Kids, 2017 | Series: US landmarks |
        Includes bibliographical references and index.

Identifiers: LCCN 2016943930 | ISBN 9781680809121 (lib. bdg.) |
        ISBN 9781680796223 (ebook) | ISBN 9781680796896 (Read-to-me ebook)

Subjects: LCSH: Martin Luther King Jr. Memorial--Juvenile literature. |
        Washington (D.C.)--Buildings, structures, etc.--Juvenile literature.

Classification: DDC 975.3--dc23

LC record available at http://lccn.loc.gov/2016943930

Table of Contents

Martin Luther King Jr. Memorial

It **honors** Martin Luther King Jr.

He was a leader.

4

He wanted peace.

He fought for **civil rights**.

9

He was shot. He died.

He was 39 years old.

11

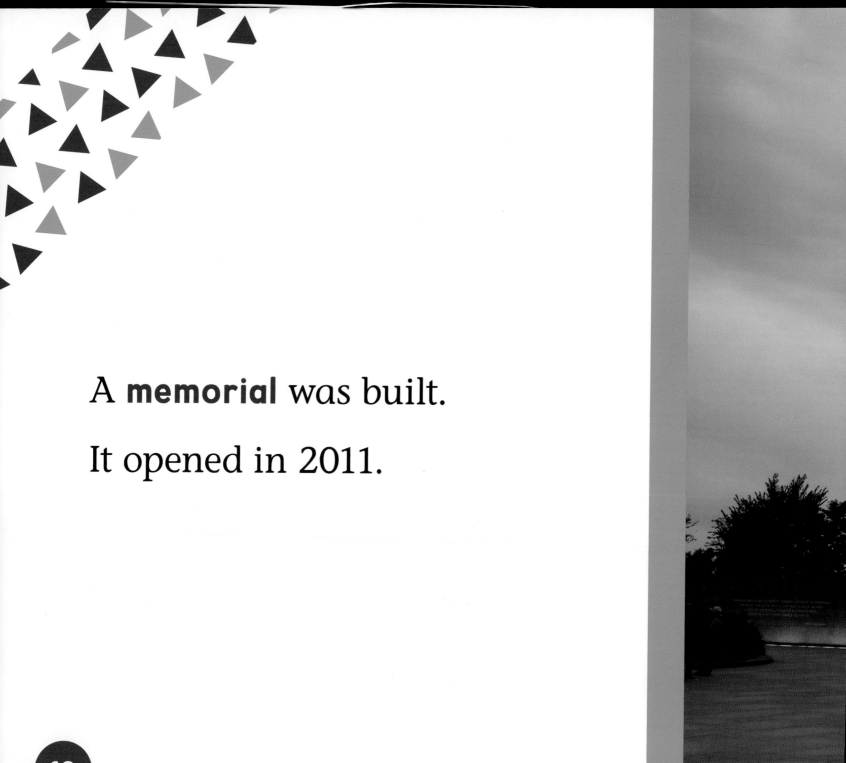

A **memorial** was built.

It opened in 2011.

It took two years to build.

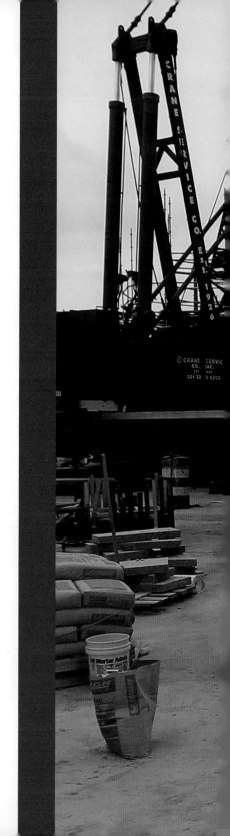

15

It is in Washington, D.C.

It has a statue of him.

It is 30 feet (9.1 m) tall.

It is called "The Stone of Hope."

OUT OF THE MOUNTAIN OF DESPAIR,
A STONE OF HOPE

Parts of the Memorial

inscription wall

Mountain of Despair

Martin Luther King Jr.

Stone of Hope

Glossary

civil rights
rights to personal freedom, especially for an individual or minority group.

honor
to show great respect and admiration toward someone.

memorial
something made to preserve the memory of a person or event.

Index

abdokids.com

Use this code to log on to abdokids.com and access crafts, games, videos, and more!

Abdo Kids Code:
UMK9121